I0188765

Thinking About Homeschool?

"What About Sports?"

Learning to learn with each other

Written by Robin and Tony Weaver

Art by Polina Hrytskova

Inspirational credits to The Hill Country Homeschoolers and Golden Eagle Charter School, Sweet Berry Farm and Hunter Orchards, Harmony School for the Arts and Mount Shasta Art Bus, Mount Shasta Martial Arts Program and AcroTex Gymnastics, YMCA and Mount Shasta Fitness Center, US Forest Service and State Parks, Botanical Gardens and City Parks, Safaris and Zoos, Museums, Universities, Family, Friends, Neighbors .....

Habitats & Homesteads

Thinking About Homeschool?
What About Sports?

Copyright 2018 © by

Habitats & Homesteads

Exploring Sustainable Solutions

All rights reserved.
No part of this book may be reproduced in any form without written permission from the publisher:

Habitats and Homesteads, LLC
507 Mill Street
Mount Shasta, CA 96067
USA
habitatsandhomesteads.com

Written by
Tony, Robin, Lily, Elder Weaver

Illustrations by
Polina Hrytskova

Habitats & Homesteads

"What About Sports?"

George, learning to be a team player.

Today is a great day! I'm with dad watching our favorite baseball team. Someday I really want to be an athlete that gets to play games in big stadiums all over the country.

ADELTA

My mom says that I have so much energy that I bounce off the walls in her house. So, we are at the youth center talking to Couch Ramirez about signing me up for a soccer team.

It's really important to have the right shoes for the sport you are playing. Today I'm getting new cleats because my feet are too big for my old ones. Cleats help me run and stop fast when I play soccer and baseball.

We are working on passing the ball to one another and going around cones as we run up and down the field. We yell "Good Job!" when a teammate is trying hard and getting better.

We are winning our first game! Coach says they are teaching us about some weak points that we need to work on but that we are playing well. Practice is going to be hard this week.

The park is a great place to meet up with all of my homeschool friends. Phillip plays football with one of the local charter school teams and always brings a ball to toss.

Every year I come to a field day that some of the homeschool parents started. We are running relay races and playing goofy games. I've won the sack race for my age group for 3 years now!

Some of the kids at our Library Book Club brought me to a disc golf park. It's a calm day so it's easier to learn how to play for a beginner like me.

At the Homeschool Harvest Festival I am hauling heavy pumpkins to the giant slingshot. My arm muscles are going to hurt so much tomorrow. Dad always says, "No pain, no gain."

Both of my parents have basketball hoops at their houses. I'm at my mom's practicing shooting hoops during my break from math. At dad's house we like to play one-on-one.

My dad and I like to go to different places to ride our bikes together. Today we are riding 12 miles of steep trails to start building up my strength for a race. I love this park.

This is my first year playing hockey and I'm not sure if I like it. I'm not a great skater but I will stay on the team until the season is over. Mom and Dad are happy that I want to see it through to the end.

I told you I was a bad skater. I fell on my arm in a weird way and now the doctor told me that I have a bad sprain. At least it's not broken but it sure does hurt.

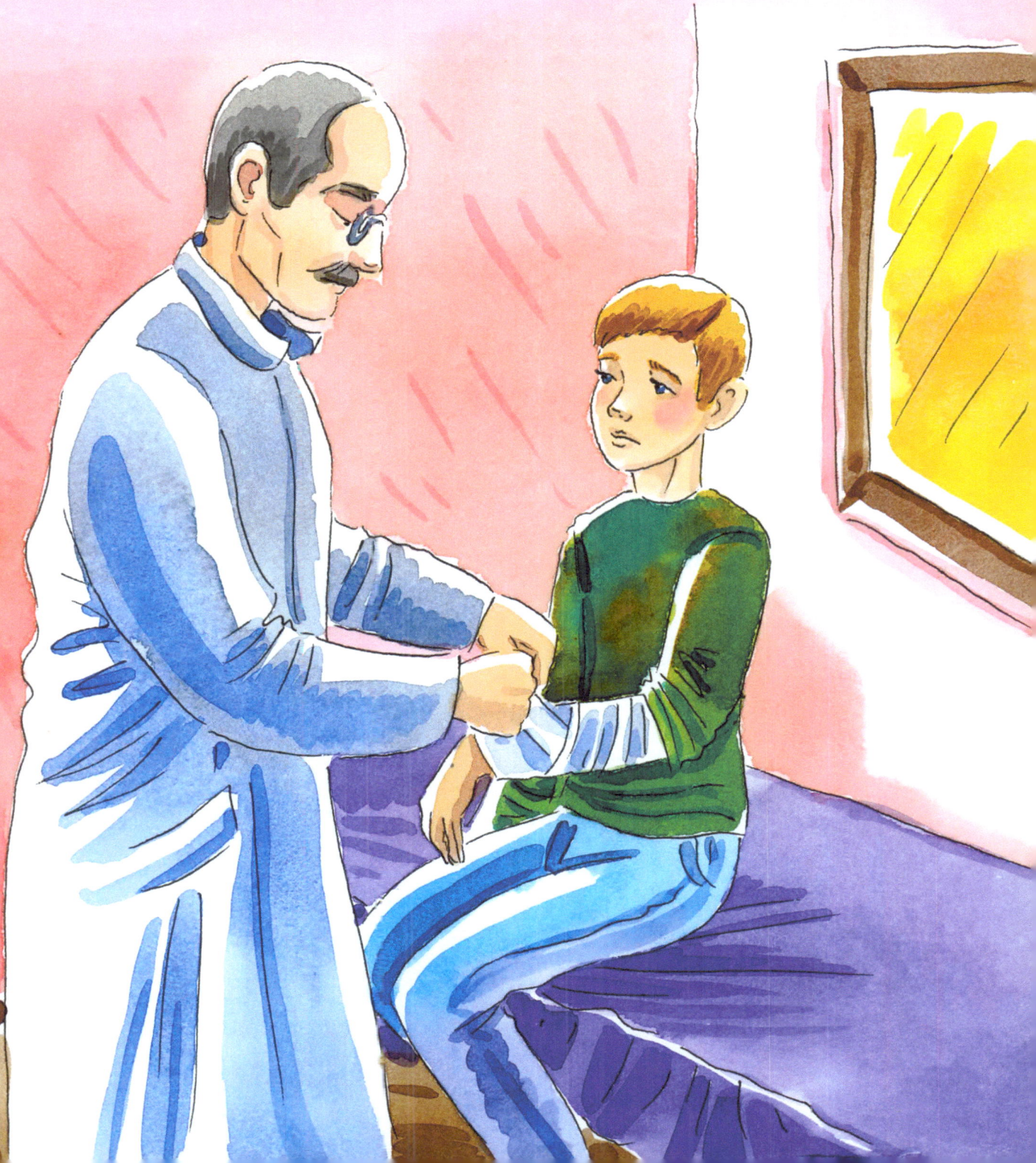

We are at a nearby frozen lake to ice skate and play in the snow.
I'm glad my wrist feels better because Jack and I are getting extra
cocoa for helping shovel snow off the ice.

My stepdad Jake brought me snowboarding today. He is the head of the Snow Patrol that helps people when they get hurt in the mountains. Jake taught me how to snowboard when I was really little.

Today I am at my martial arts class. Jake and my mom think that it is a good idea for me to learn about self defense. I like the exercise but I don't really like hitting and kicking people.

We came to see my stepsister play in a basketball game at the high school this evening. I'm learning a lot of moves by watching her team. She's really good!

I wrote a report on Michael Jordan for the Book Club this month. He is one of the best basketball players ever. I can be that good at a sport as long as I work hard.

These otters that live at the aquarium are so funny! We are laughing really hard watching them race and play with each other.With practice, I will be able to swim that fast.

I'm finally getting a chance to try out boogie boarding during our group trip to the beach. Some good surfers are showing me how to catch a wave and ride it into shore.

I was nominated to take trash bags across the water while we are cleaning up the river on Earth Day. I'm glad that I've been exercising because the current is strong, but I am stronger.

My dad comes over after work everyday to train with me for a triathlon. He is really good at teaching me to pace myself in a race. I'm glad that I get to see him more often lately.

Catrina is telling me all about how the Maypole is the center of a giant circle called an axis. She is always talking about how everything is about science and math. I think it looks like a fun game.

My parents are really strict about how much sugar I eat because I am already hyper. On special occasions, like my mom's birthday today, I am allowed to eat more sweet treats.

Every year the homeschool group plants a big garden. My job today is to move compost with the wheelbarrow. I'm giving lots of kids rides on the way back to the pile. It's a great workout and lots of fun too!

This day is finally here! I am competing in my very first triathlon!
I've been training for this a really long time and I feel fast.

Grandpa says that fishing is a sport. I guess you could call sitting in a boat a sport. Grandpa is going to teach me how to clean a fish if we ever catch one.

Do you remember that lake that we shoveled in winter for ice skating? It's summer and is so hot that everyone is out swimming in the cool water. I am working on my flips and dives off of the dock.

I am playing baseball on a team at the youth center again this year.
Coach makes us take a knee when he is talking because it helps us to
listen better and show respect. Baseball is my favorite sport.

Dad takes me to a professional baseball game every year. This game is a dream come true! I'm so excited to be down by the field talking to one of my favorite players. It's official, I want to play professional baseball.

www.ingramcontent.com/pod-product-compliance
Lightning Source LLC
Chambersburg PA
CBHW042056040426
42447CB00003B/243